Denis Thorpe on home ground

Denis Thorpe on home ground

LOWRY PRESS

Return of a prisoner of war, Mansfield Woodhouse, Nottinghamshire, 1953. Trooper Ben Baugh went to the Korean war where he was captured and imprisoned for two years. On his return he received a hero's welcome in the streets.

As a general rule for press photographers, it helps to be unobtrusive. One of the reasons Denis Thorpe is such a great photographer is that he is almost invisible.

Seeing some press photographers at work these days you feel theirs is a lifestyle choice as much as a vocation. They come in standard issue bomber jacket and jeans, lassoed with multiple cameras, each lens longer than the lens before. Some need a small mini-bus to transport all their gear. The flash equipment alone could light a small cathedral.

Not Denis. Small, bald, soberly dressed in suit and tie or dark brown raincoat. A pair of glasses perched halfway down his nose. An old bag over his shoulder. Softly spoken. You could look at him for quite some time before noticing a camera. Denis Thorpe and Jane Bown must be the two most physically anonymous photographers of their generation.

I have seen Denis photographing a street scene in Moscow without even realising he was at work. His beloved Leica was at stomach height, his eyes elsewhere altogether. You had to watch closely to see his hands silently focus the lens on the picture he wanted. You never heard the click.

But, of course, it is the eye that matters most. It is the ability to compose a picture - to see patterns, symbols, drama and movement, whether it is in a landscape or a face. You can work a lifetime behind the lens without having that eye. Denis has it.

You knew that every time Denis was out on a job, he would come back with something special. As a reporter he always illuminated whatever you were working on and added a depth you couldn't achieve with words alone. As an editor you knew a Denis Thorpe image would hold up any page. You couldn't be in safer hands.

Most journalism is – literally – here today and gone tomorrow. Most words are soon forgotten, most images fade from the mind. So it is startling to see a life's work such as this collected in one volume. It is not simply the freshness and directness of so many of the pictures. It is the realisation that a lifetime of reportage can come together in an utterly coherent body of work, all informed by the same humanity, integrity and that sense of quiet, unobtrusive observance. It is a very great achievement.

Alan Rusbridger, Editor, the *Guardian*

Denis Thorpe comes over as a quiet almost self-effacing character. He would probably say this comes of years of trying to be unobtrusive, of sliding into the background, the better to capture an event, as a master photojournalist. But colleagues will attest to his toughness and tenacity. The qualities, compositional and technical of his photography show him to be unstinting in his demands on himself. Flaubert wrote of genius being a protracted patience *une longue patience* – during which you tease away at perfection. The heat of the moment means often for the photojournalist, you have to bring to bear lots of experience, second guessing or you have to lie in wait. The demands of deadlines can militate against this and part of Denis' genius is that he was able to combine both his personal demands of a good photograph and that of the picture desk. Many have seen other photographers' idioms at work in Denis' photography and it is a fact he has great admiration for others – but it is the contention of this book and The Lowry's exhibition that this quiet man is very much his own man, a strong and characterful portrayer of identity and humanity. It is a privilege for The Lowry to celebrate his contribution to how we see ourselves.

David Alston, Galleries Director, The Lowry

Page 1
Mansfield, Nottinghamshire, 1950.

Page 2
Waiting for diphtheria immunisation, Mansfield, 1954.

I recall something that Denis Thorpe remarked when I first met him: "I'm so fortunate to have spent my whole career shooting in black and white." What might seem a limitation to some photographers has been his pride and joy. His craft, honed to perfection, has been the monochrome image produced for the pages of a newspaper. It is a demanding art, not unlike that of the engraver – with which it has some things in common. Engravings and press photographs must both stand out on the page. Their makers sometimes use artistic devices such as shooting into the light, for instance, to define the subject with a sharpness that makes it jump out from its background, for the rotogravure press often muddies the delicacy of half-tones, particularly on the poorer-quality newsprint of the past. Thorpe became a master at using the medium's deficiencies to make what he calls "my sort of photographs". A Denis Thorpe image is one in which the qualities of composition, of tonal control and human interest are uppermost. The result is photographs which stand full comparison with the best work of his mentors and heroes – Bill Brandt, Henri Cartier-Bresson, Robert Doisneau, Bert Hardy.

The pressure to create a strong or emotive image to accompany a news or feature item can sometimes result in a type of pictorial compression which is exploitative or voyeuristic. But these are terms that could never be applied to a photograph made by Thorpe. A gentle and quietly spoken man, he has always considered himself "a photojournalist" rather than as a press photographer. This is not to denigrate the "press" but more to emphasise a commitment to making photographs that offer an honest and compassionate depiction of a situation and the people involved in it. They are the fruit of what was often a longer and deeper look at the subject than is typical in news reporting.

This patient approach comes across in all of Thorpe's work, but is seen at its most poignant in his portraits. The sitter is hardly ever confronted in full-face, usually arranged as if comfortably occupying their surroundings. Thorpe's portraits embody a complicity that offers an honest account of the person, one in which they would have no trouble recognising themselves. Documentary photography of the type practised by Thorpe is often described as seeking deeper truths, but this sometimes produces images that can be aggressive in their "compassion". A better term for Thorpe's approach to photojournalism might be to call it the work of an *honest witness*, whose pictures tell us something about the maker at the same time as they inform us of their subject matter.

During the 20th century, the work of the documentary photographer

an honest witness

by Peter Hamilton

Rudolf Nureyev,
Manchester, 1981.

Sealdah railway station,
Calcutta, 1977.

(not a good term, perhaps, but one which certainly encompasses many honourable pursuits that have included that of the photojournalist) has been seen in many lights, but in broad terms there is no doubt that its cultural standing *has* changed, probably for the better. At the beginning of the century, photographs were just starting to appear on the pages of newspapers and magazines. The people who made them were looked upon as enterprising craftspeople, and sometimes achieved a certain celebrity as a result. Starting in the late 1920s and early 1930s, a revolution had taken place in the illustrated press and new imprints were rushing off the presses – *Vu* in France, *Life* in the USA, *Picture Post* in Britain. They called upon a new breed of popular artist, the illustrative photographer or photojournalist (as Americans soon called them) to create the visual materials that would cover their pages. Stories of human interest, of everyday life, had come to the fore and a new form of photographic representation – humanism – rapidly achieved visual dominance. Its practitioners frequently created their picture stories around the ordinary individual in his or her daily life, and used the new technology of small, light, handheld cameras, such as the Leica and the Rolleiflex, to get in touch with the rhythms of everyday life.

Humanist photojournalism serviced the mass-readership magazines of the era until television began to cut a swathe through their markets in the mid 1950s. It produced its stars and iconic works – W. Eugene Smith and his "Country Doctor" story for *Life* in 1948, Robert Doisneau and his Parisian lovers, another picture story made for *Life* in 1950 – are only a couple of examples of this movement. They were popular, they dealt with easily recognised issues, and they offered what can be seen as an "inclusive" image of post-war society. The realisation that such work might be seen as an important art form in its own right came about through the work of Alfred Steichen, photographic curator of the Museum of Modern Art from 1946 to 1962, and the leading protagonist in the great *Family of Man* exhibition that toured the USA and the rest of the world in the mid to late 1950s.

The substantial body of Denis Thorpe's photographs should be viewed against the backdrop of such trends. Born in Mansfield in 1932, where his father was an iron-foundry worker, the young Thorpe first dreamt of a career as a reporter, as a writer rather than a photographer. Serious illness kept him out of school for a couple of years, but he was encouraged to write by a sympathetic teacher and success at this form of self-expression led to him badgering the local paper for a job when he left school in 1948. As he told me once, "The *Mansfield Reporter* gave me a job but they said, 'If you

come here you'll have to do everything.' I remember rushing home to tell my mother, and she asked me how much I would be earning. But I didn't know or care!"

He had the good fortune to work with the paper's photographer, a man with aesthetic aspirations: "He was not a proper press photographer, he was fascinated by *Picture Post*: he even had a Zeiss Contax like Bert Hardy's." This was at a time when virtually all other press photographers in Britain were using plate cameras and flash-guns. Thorpe's mentor was a generous man, for he allowed him to use the prized 35mm Contax, even to take it home. With it Thorpe made some of the family photographs shown here which include a fine portrait of his father, and some highly atmospheric images such as the couple walking the wet Mansfield streets, seen through his bedroom window (page 1).

This was work which might in other circumstances have appeared in the great reportage magazines of the era, such as *Picture Post* or *Life*, which Thorpe was by then avidly consuming. The dearth of photographic books in the Mansfield public library led him into the history of art section, where he discovered the French Impressionists. He was intrigued by the way in which painters such as Degas had created compositions in which the frame of the image was used in new and exciting ways.

The real turning point in Thorpe's life came in 1950. The Creswell Colliery disaster took the lives of 80 miners, and Thorpe was sent by his paper to cover it. "The enormity of it really struck home. I photographed

the people who had come to wait at the pit-head, relatives and friends of those underground, and I began to realise that photography could have an impact which words could not." Shortly after, Thorpe was obliged to leave the paper to do his National Service, but made sure that he held on to his negatives of this event. They are pictures which record, with compassion and respect, the despair and grief of those left waiting for news of loved ones.

Returning to Mansfield in 1953, Thorpe had begun to see that his future career might lie in photojournalism. During stints on a number of regional titles, in Northampton and Birmingham, he started to whittle out his own photo-stories from the daily grind of the staff-photographer's duties on a local paper, and would regularly assemble this work and take it to London in the hope of getting a job with a national daily or even *Picture Post*.

He had purchased his own Zeiss Contax, with fast f1.5 Sonnar 50mm lens, although the press work he was paid to do brought with it the obligation to use bulky 9x12cm VN, Plaubel Makina and MPP 5"x4" plate cameras. "The real problem was that the papers were just not set up to use 35mm. The enlargers were converted horizontal process cameras made for 15"x12" plates. If you brought a 35mm film into the darkroom they would

process it in the paper developer! It was hopeless." The prevailing techniques were outdated but simple. Press photographs existed only to support a news story, so the photographer went out with a 9x12cm camera, a dozen single plateholders and a flashgun with PF60 bulbs. A single, defining image would be made, the plates rushed back for rapid development and then printed, wet, for the picture editor to make his choice of what would appear in the newspaper.

Despite these limitations Thorpe was determined to plough his own furrow, and showed his work to those in London who could appreciate it. They included Norman Hall, editor of *Photography* magazine and later picture editor of *The Times*, who encouraged several young photojournalists and published Thorpe's work alongside that of Philip Jones Griffiths in 1956. Picture Post was by this stage moribund, and its most illustrious editor, Tom Hopkinson, had left to work for the *News Chronicle*. He too liked Thorpe's work, but suggested that "you are not using many lenses!" At one point in the 1950s Denis tried to freelance, selling his pictures through an agency (Pictorial Press), but found it hard to survive.

The lowly status of the photographer in the newspapers of this era irked Thorpe. In 1957 he found a job on the staff of the *Daily Mail*, based in the Manchester office (at that time there were several regional editions of the national daily, with offices in the North, Scotland and Ireland). But the 35mm Contax had to go, replaced by a Rolleiflex which made Denis the first photojournalist in Manchester to use the camera which had become by the late 1950s the synonym of the press photographer. "I had been up to London to see the *Family of Man* exhibition. I still had this beautiful Contax, but I thought "they'll never let me use it", so I sold it and bought the Rollei for £135. I came back with that and all these images from the 'Family of Man' in the subconscious. Yet I couldn't afford to buy the catalogue – and this was the finest work I'd ever seen."

Thorpe's love of his medium made him an avid collector of photographic books, and ensured that he went to see the rare exhibitions of photography which occurred in the 1950s, including the first Cartier-Bresson show in 1957. As Norman Hall pointed out in the pages of *Photography*, British photojournalism did not die with *Picture Post* in 1957, and the early 1960s saw the emergence of new publications, and the first signs of an increasing public fascination with the genre. Denis Thorpe was close in spirit to the group Martin Harrison has branded the Young Meteors. Their work testified to the vitality of another tradition of press photography, rooted in a deep awareness of the best European and

Traditional cockle fisherman,
The Wash, 1988.

American work. He took opportunities which would allow him greater scope whenever they appeared, such as the Cod War of 1958-59 when he spent six weeks on a deep-sea trawler in the Arctic. "There were no expenses! Nobody else wanted to do it, but I thought it was wonderful. I bought a lot of my favourite FP3 film for myself, so that I could do a picture story of my own as well as the news pictures. But apart from Norman Hall who used it in *Photography Year Book* nobody was interested in the picture essay."

Initially Denis worked at the *Mail* with another "young meteor", the talented but almost forgotten Graham Finlayson (1932-99), who shared many of Thorpe's aspirations for their work. Finlayson soon moved on to the *Guardian*, but when he left that journal to pursue a freelance career in the early 1960s, Thorpe felt his chance had come to take up a career with the only British newspaper congenial to his own approach. "I was offered the job and was absolutely delighted, because the *Guardian* gave you the chance to do your own thing. But before I could take it up the offer was withdrawn because a staff photographer in London wanted to come back to the Northern office. I was deeply disappointed."

The chance to move to the *Guardian* would come eleven years later in 1974. By this time Thorpe had amassed very considerable experience, and had seen the final bastions of conservative practice taken over by the 35mm camera. His work had taken him to the burgeoning conflict in Northern Ireland, as well to scenes of strife on his own doorstep. Despite the vicissitudes of such work, Thorpe remained ever vigilant about the pictorial quality of the photographs he made. Throughout this career he had made it a point to try to control, wherever possible, how his pictures were used. "I always made sure that I developed the film, and if I could do so I would also supervise making the prints. If possible I would ensure that the picture editor got a 16"x12" print from me, so that they didn't have to use the poorer quality wire picture."

Thorpe insists that the period he worked as staff photographer on the *Guardian* were the "golden years" of newspaper photojournalism. Economic and technological changes in newspaper production have since changed the way in which photographs can be made and used, and they are much more likely now to be seen as graphic adjuncts to the text. It is a tribute to the enlightened stance of the newspaper that Thorpe's humane and expressive style was used to such great effect by a publication which encouraged him to shoot around a subject. When he was sent to India for three weeks in 1977 it was without specific instructions: "They said, 'Just go,

do your own thing.' Can you imagine what a burden that is?"

Such indulgence by his employers allowed Thorpe's natural flair to flourish, and the time it permitted him to spend on a single picture always seems to have paid dividends. It can be seen in the making of what is, arguably, his best-known image. Thorpe made the photograph of Hebden Bridge on a snowy day in 1978. It took many hours of waiting for Thorpe to get the shot he needed, his camera set up on a tripod, with the shape defined in the viewfinder, but the crucial light conditions that would give the right degree of contrast and tonal separation were lacking until the final decisive moment when everything came together for one extraordinary photograph.

Denis Thorpe has always worked within a genre that can be described as humanist-pictorialist, crafting a body of work from the daily tasks of reportage. Perhaps, at the end of the day, it is not the form of an artist's work that defines its quality, but the energy and skill devoted, over a long period, to its achievement. There might be a sense in which Thorpe could have been placed anywhere in the world with the assurance that he would have brought back a group of visually satisfying photographs. He did so many times, but this book must needs concentrate on those made within the British Isles. For his best work seems to have been made while he was in close touch with the people and places with which he maintains the deepest sympathies, on home ground.

Lowry

L S Lowry about to receive
academic honours from
Salford University, 1975.

Paintings, paints and
brushes at The Elms,
L S Lowry's home, 1972.

Mr Lowry's hats and coats, 1976.
It was discovered much later
that the artist had already
sketched almost precisely the
same image in 1965.

The hallway and stairs at
The Elms, 1976. The day after
Mr. Lowry died Denis Thorpe
decided to pay homage and
drove past The Elms only to
discover all the effects being
removed by Securicor. He
managed to persuade people
that it seemed they were about
to dismantle history, and so,
fortunately, was allowed to
make a unique record of the
interior of the house before
other paintings and personal
treasures were removed.

family

Laura Thorpe, Mansfield, 1950.

Bathing after work at the iron foundry, Mansfield, 1950.

Laura Thorpe. Mansfield, 1950.

Thomas Thorpe. Iron moulder,
Mansfield, 1950.

people

Nuns at a religious conference,
Manchester, 1959.

Yates's Wine Lodge,
Blackpool, 1976.

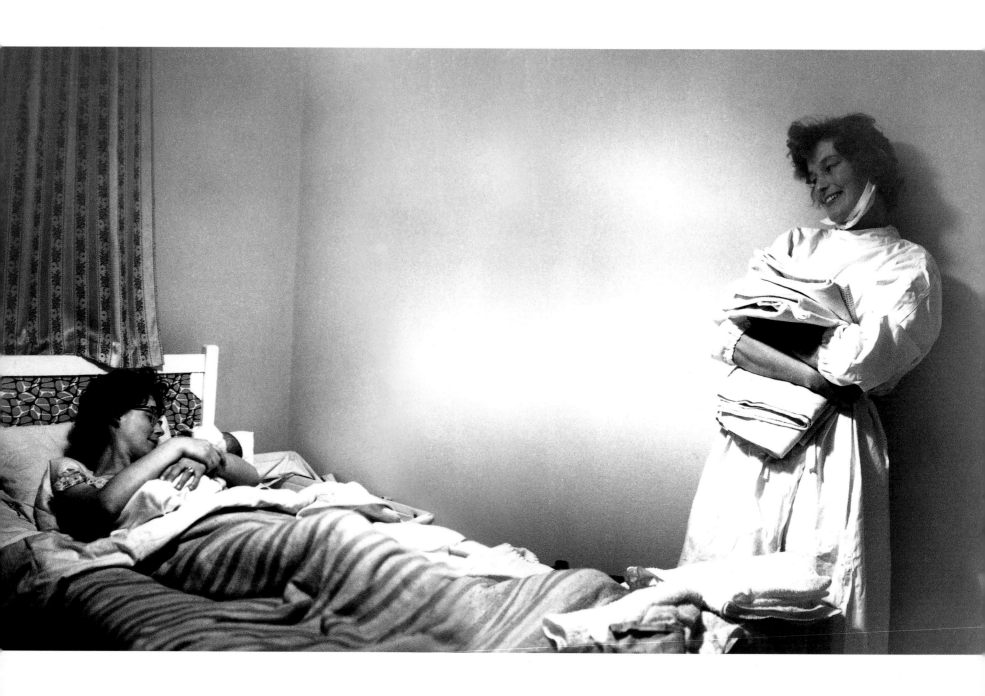

Midwife, mother and baby
Cheshire, 1961.

Walker Art Gallery
Liverpool, 1992.

Suzuki Violin School,
Evesham, 1978.

Backyard, central
Birmingham, 1956.

Previous page
Pierhead, Liverpool, 1976.

Playground, Bury Grammar
School, Lancashire, 1990.

The M6 in Cheshire. Opening day
of the Thelwall Viaduct over the
Manchester Ship Canal, 1963.

Francis Lee and Rodney Marsh,
Maine Road, Manchester, 1972.

Old Trafford, Manchester, 1958.
Young Manchester United
supporters show high emotions
- this was the first match after
the Munich Disaster.

Residents, The Crescent,
Hulme, Manchester, 1978.

Shelter Office, Birmingham, 1978. A homeless couple having been evicted await rehousing.

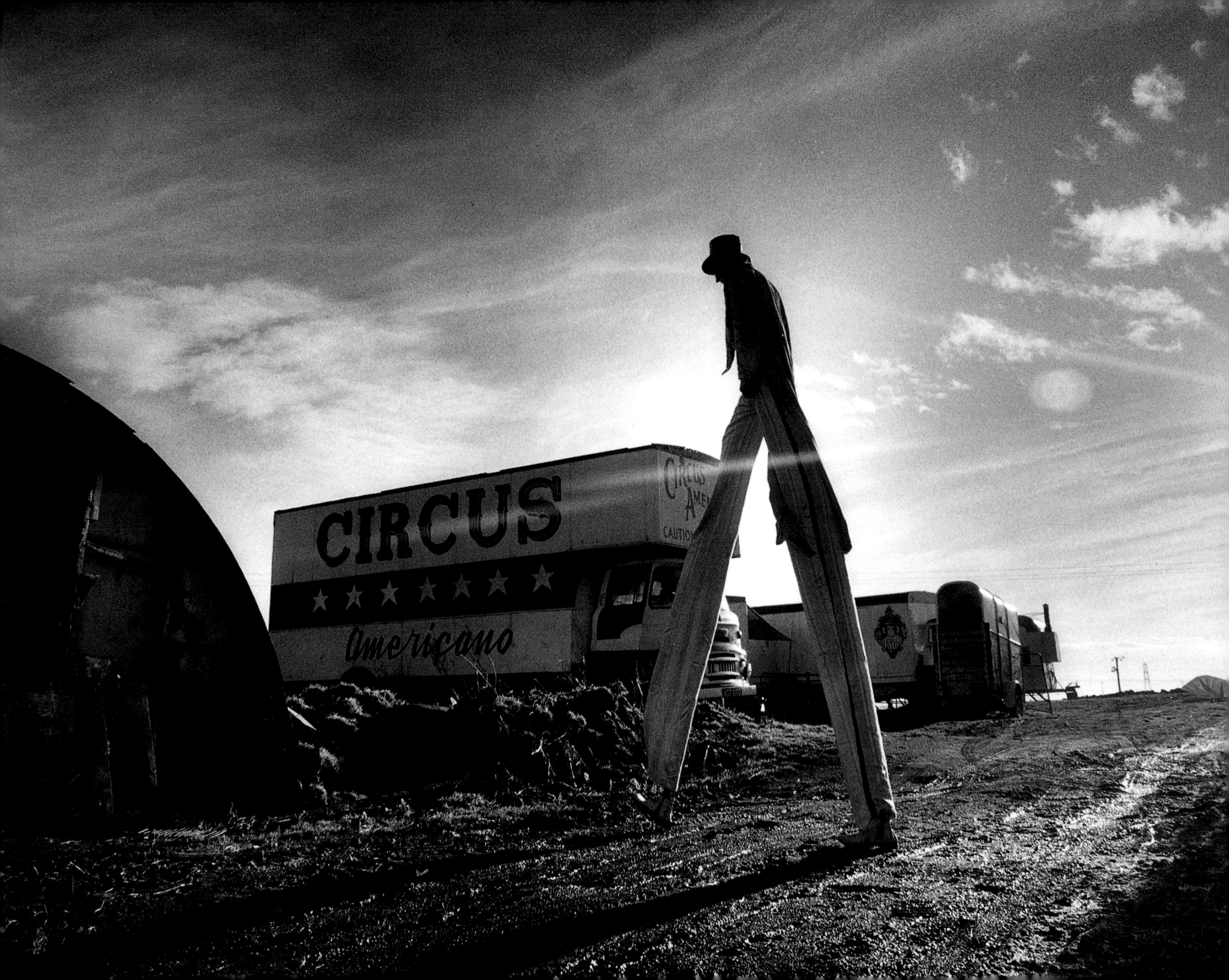
CIRCUS
Americano
CIRCUS
CAUTION

Circus Americano in winter
quarters, Yorkshire, 1976.

Circus folk visit a sick friend.
Blackpool, 1974.

Interior of North Leverton
Windmill, Nottinghamshire,
1975.

Brian Keenan, Co Mayo, Ireland 1992. After his release, the former Beirut hostage went to a remote location to write *An Evil Cradling*. He is depicted in the freedom of the wide landscape, and in a portrait which shows the seeming isolation of imprisonment, but was actually Brian deep in thought in a bar late at night.

Denis Thorpe considers this assignment (which also includes colour) produced one of his most memorable and rewarding picture stories.

work

The *Lincoln City*, a Grimsby steam trawler in the Arctic off Iceland, during the Cod War, 1958. A tense time for the skipper.

Preparing nets, 1958.

Fishing off Iceland, 1958.

Aberdeen harbour, 1958.

Traditional cockle fishermen,
The Wash, 1988.

Ashington, Northumberland, 1982. A miner taking in concessionary coal.

Manton Colliery, Nottinghamshire,1984. This miner had arrived on the surface after the first shift at the end of the strike.

Miners' strike, 1984. A miner's
child at the Welfare Hall,
Askern, South Yorkshire.

Creswell Colliery disaster,
Derbyshire, 1950. The families
of miners gathered at the
pithead waiting to hear the
terrible news. Eighty miners
had died underground.

Creswell Colliery, Derbyshire,
1974, The coal face.

Shipyard workforce,
Barrow-in-Furness, Cumbria,
1992. Roll-out of the first
Trident submarine.

Giuseppe Lund, Blacksmith
and Artist, Ironbridge,
Shropshire, 1980.

Stone-quarrymen,
Yorkshire, 1992.

The famous streamlined steam locomotive, *Sir Nigel Gresley*, Shilton, Co Durham, 1975. It was the 150th anniversary of the Liverpool-Manchester Railway, the world's first passenger line.

Restored water-wheel mechanism, Quarry Bank Mill, Styal, Cheshire, 1991.

Shoe museum, Rossendale,
Lancashire, 1991.

Heysham Power Station under
construction, Lancashire, 1983.

Mossley, Lancashire, 1972.

Cotton-mill roof, Nelson,
Lancashire, 1978.

strife

Army patrol, Belfast, 1980.

Schoolboy, Belfast, 1971.
Journalists would often visit
schools and the children
were asked to talk about
current events.

Army patrol, Belfast, 1980.

Divis Flats complex,
Belfast, 1980.

Housing estate, North Dublin,
during Irish elections, 1981.

Law Courts, Belfast, 1980.

Belfast, 1976.

Belfast, 1971. With great dignity, Peter Gallagher carries the tiny coffin of his 18-month-old daughter Angela, killed when caught in terrorist gunfire.

Belfast, 1976.

Londonderry, 1985.

Strangeways Prison siege, 1990.

Police helicopter on first night of the siege.

city

Shipyard cranes,
Sunderland, 1980.

Manchester Ship Canal.
Runcorn-Widnes Bridge, 1995.

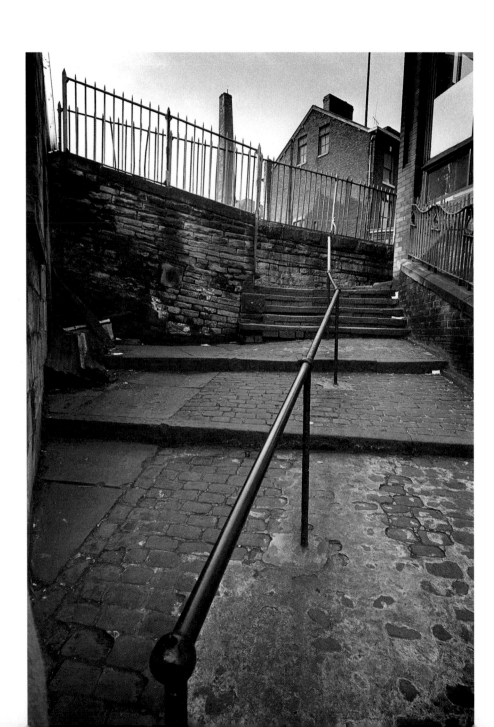

Steps in Stockport, 1970.

Holmfirth, Yorkshire, 1983.

Street in Salford, 1979.
Terraced housing waiting
for demolition.

Camel Laird shipyard,
Birkenhead, 1988.

Power station and terraced
housing, Middleton,
Lancashire, 1976.

Policeman in St George's Square,
Liverpool, 1990.

Edgeley, Stockport, 1970.

Kelvin Flats complex,
Sheffield, 1987.

Midland Hotel,
Morecambe, 1975.

Cotton Mill, Stockport, 1970.

Burnley, Lancashire, 1977.

country

Goodrich Castle,
Herefordshire. 1993.

Crofter, Applecross,
Scotland, 1980.

Slopes of Mam Tor,
Derbyshire, 1977.

Hebden Bridge, Yorkshire, 1978.

Appleby Horse Fair,
Cumbria, 1974.

Appleby Horse Fair,
Cumbria, 1990.

Appleby Horse Fair, Cumbria, 1990 (both images).

Arbor Low Prehistoric Stone
Circle, Derbyshire, 1975.

Copse, Snowdonia, Gwynedd,
Wales, 1974.

Lleyn Peninsula,
Gwynedd, Wales, 1984.

Lake Bala, Gwynedd,
Wales, 1976.

Ribblehead Viaduct, the
Settle-Carlisle Railway, North
Yorkshire, 1986.

Deserted cottage, Nant Gwrtheyrn, Gwynedd, Wales, 1974.

Birdoswald, Hadrian's Wall, Northumberland, 1995.

Liverpool Garden Festival,
Landscaped Hill designed by
Paul Young. 1984.

Isle of Barra, Scotland, 1984.

South Stack Lighthouse,
Holy Island, Anglesey, 1978.

Field patterns, Leigh,
Lancashire, 1977.

Rushup Edge, Derbyshire, 1974.

Ray Dent, hill shepherd,
Weardale, Co Durham, 1977.

Cumbrian hill shepherd, 1990.

Weardale, Co Durham, hill
shepherd, Ian Dent, 1977.

Dedicated to my wife Patricia, my sons and daughters,
and in memory of my mother and father.

Acknowledgements

The author wishes to thank the following for their help and encouragement

The Lowry: David Alston, Emma Anderson, Charu Vallabhbhai,
Lindsay Brooks, Edward Daniels.

Roger Sears of Lowry Press, Jon Allan at Pocknell Studio.

The *Guardian*: Alan Rusbridger, Eamonn McCabe, Don McPhee, David Ward,
Jane Breslin, John Course, Brian Crook, Martin Wainwright, Ian Wright.

Daily Mail: Paul Silva, David Sheppard.

Potteries Museum and Art Gallery: Alan Taylor.

Robert Waterhouse, Peter Hamilton, John Chillingworth, Roger Grayson,
and everyone who has generously given their time for research. Most of my
photography has been done at speed on the wing, so to all the people who
have allowed me into their lives, however briefly, my special thanks are due.

pp. 27, 28/29, 59, 66/67 © *Daily Mail*, courtesy Associated Newspapers Ltd

Publishing and editorial direction: Roger Sears
Edited by Michael Leitch
Designed by Jon Allan at Pocknell Studio

Published by the Lowry Press on the occasion of the exhibition
Denis Thorpe: On Home Ground
The Lowry
From 5 May 2001

The Lowry
Pier 8, Salford Quays, Salford M5 2AZ
Telephone: 44 (0) 161 876 2020 Fax: 44 (0) 161 876 2021
www.thelowry.com

First published 2001
© The Lowry Centre Limited
All images other than those listed above © Denis Thorpe/The *Guardian*
A CIP catalogue record for this book is available from The British Library
ISBN 1 902970 15 2
Originated in Singapore and printed and bound in Italy by Imago

on home ground is published in association with *The***GuardianNorth**